I Cried

Last Night

(Sharing

a Loss)

by

Bob Mullin

PEACE,
Bob

Special thanks to

Linda Lucas

for the cover design

and invaluable help.

I

I cried last night
from the hurt

And this morning
the smile of the sun
seems to heal
the day's frost.

II

I feel empty
    as if
    I have lost all.

It is a deep sense
    of having nothing.

But does not emptiness
    provide an openness!

III

You try to hold on!
You try to forget!
Whatever you do;
     it doesn't work.
I've come to realize
     that the only way
     to face a loss
     is to look
     straight at it
     and be thankful
     that you are aware
     it is a loss.
And that you have loved!

IV

To lose a loved one
whether
by death or separation
is a tragedy
of the heart.
It brings to the forefront
the ache
of our need
to be loved.
But it also brings to light
the ache
of our gift
to love.

(con't)

We miss both
  the fulfillment
     of our need
  and
  the expression
     of our gift.

V

I went to
two funerals tonight,
one of a person,
one of a relationship,
one I knew about
one I had to find out about.

Death is really a part of life,
but only
when we look right at it.
To see it and accept it
        is to go on living.
Not to accept it
        is not to live;
                (con't)

for then
it's only make-believe.

One day in the woods
    I came across
    a dead sparrow.
I sat for a while
    and wished
    it had not died.
But only when
    I accepted the death
      of the sparrow
    did I get up
    and go on living.

VI

It isn't happening.
It just can't be.
It just seems like it.

           I deny it.

It's not fair!
Damn it!
Why me!
I don't deserve this!

           I'm angry.

Maybe it just looks like it.
Maybe it's a
misunderstanding.
Maybe if I just wait a while.
Maybe if I just change a
little.

           I'll bargain.
           (con't)

It's not right.
What did I do to deserve
this?
Why should this happen to
me?
Why me?

               I'm depressed.

It is happening.
It just is.
It is.
Let it be.

               I accept.

VII

All the booths are empty.
　　　　So feels my soul.
But if I close the door
　　　　　　to hurt,
　no one can come in;
　nor can I go out.

To lock the door to hurt
　　is to lock it to all else.

A garden would not be
　a real garden
　without some weeds.

(con't)

A flower grows
  only in the spot
  that could hold a weed.

So don't be afraid
      of weeds;
they surround the flower.

The sun shines on all.

VIII

I will answer
  your question,
    "Why?"

But first
    sit down
    and watch me
    draw the wind.

18

IX

Confusion
    is a gift,
        inviting you
            to turn
            to someone.

X

Is it not
in the stillness of winter
    that I feel
    the rush of spring?
Is it not
 in the death of fall
    that I understand
    the life of summer?
To make a year,
    does it not take
    all the seasons?

Because I feel my hurt
    I am able to feel yours.
            (con't)

It is in the sharing
      of the loss
      that we gain.

It is not the loss
      nor the gain;
      it is the sharing.
It is not just one season;
      it is the year.

It is sharing
      all seasons
      of the year.

XI

I didn't know you knew
     about my hurting.
I appreciated the gentleness
   with which
    you approached me.

The way you stood by me
    made me feel warm
    and fuzzy.
I hope I can do
the same for you
    when you're hurting.

I hope that
          (con't)

we can be ourselves
with each other.
I hope,
and for that I am grateful.

It is a tremendous gift,
people like you
who give me
reason to hope.

XII

I was hurting and angry.
So I called a friend.

He did not give me
      comfort:
      no answers,
      no bandages.

But he was there
at the other end
      of the phone
when I needed him.

I thanked him for that.

XIII

The joy of sharing
The sorrow of separation
The anger of hurt
The love of healing.

Each is a leaf
    on the same tree
    that, today,
    reaches
    a little more
    for the warmth
    of the sun.

XIV

My dear friend
We have spent the night
    walking our paths
    together.

The valleys
    and the mountains
    blend together
    on the horizon,
    as I know
    you are my friend.
You will not walk my path
for me,
nor I for you.

(con't)

But we do not walk alone.

For we are
   in each other's heart.

XV

I wish I could help you
      to understand,
        but I know I can't.
Sometimes
it's just too heavy
for anyone to carry alone.

I can't really explain it
because
I don't understand it either.
It is not
the weight of the load;
it's the height of the sky.
Maybe I can't explain it
                    (con't)

nor even understand it;
but one thing I can,
and will do,
is share it with you.

XVI

It was a moment
that was meant to happen,
as much as
a leaf is meant to fall,
a bird is meant to fly.

XVII

The beauty
　　of the driftwood
　　needs
　　the smoothing hands
　　of the mighty ocean
　　　　and
　　the warming heart
　　of the gentle beach.
Is not our beauty
　　sculptured
　　in the same way,
　　by hard times
　　and soft times.
Each is a gift.
Be open to both.

XVIII

A broken shell
    healed
    by the constant care
    of the ocean
    transformed into a joy
    to be heard.
Each day
    as the sky watched
    its rough edges
    were polished
    by the smoothing hands
    of the waves
    and gently placed
    on the soft sands.

(con't)

It was
  as I walked these sands,
  my memories
  being transformed
  by the constant whisper
  of the ocean,
  that the shell
  called to my eyes.
It spoke to my heart
  of hurts and healings
  of battles and truces.
It was left behind
by the receding tide
                    (con't)

along with other treasures
from the wisdom of the
deep.

It said:
from deep within you,
from beyond the ache
   call forth the strength
   to heal all wounds
   to bridge all chasms
   simply to transform
   all sorrows
   with the gentle force
   of ever-present love.

XIX

Listen to the joyful song
    of the falling leaf:

I have finished
my summer's work
of bringing the sun's life
to this tree.

I will ride the singing wind
      as I float through
the changes of life.

Maybe I'll be a toy, a fan
    for a little girl or boy.
Maybe I'll be   (con't)

the finishing touch
on your classroom wall or in
your den.

Maybe I'll join the others
    and be a pillow
        on your bed of grass.

And then I'll be some food
    hiding in the ground

till I show my soul
    next spring
        on another mighty tree.
                        (con't)

How lucky I am
    to give my life
    over and over
    and over again!

XX

The death
    of the caterpillar
    gives birth
    to the life
    of the butterfly.

The secret is
    in accepting
    the caterpillar
    we see
    the butterfly.

XXI

It is not for answers
      that we yearn.

In all its beauty
     a flower asks
     not a single question.

In sharing its gift,
     the flower
     reaches to the sky
     and rejoices.

XXII

The rain is but tears
    for your pain.

The snow is a bandage
    for your hurt.

The wind is to carry
    you along.

The sun is to warm
    your heart.

The tree gives you
    strength.

(con't)

The flower reflects
   your beauty.

The ocean shares
   your secrets.

All whispers
   My love for you.

XXIII

I was lost
in the forest of hurt,
    thinking of
    broken promises
    and
    betrayed confidences,
when a sparrow
    with a damaged wing
    hobbled
    through the trees.

And I followed him
    towards tomorrow.

XXIV

As I walked
with my head down,
I noticed a blade of grass
      pointing to the sky.
As I looked up,
      I saw a robin
      pointing to a tree.
It was a weeping willow
      singing for me.
And I smiled
      to the flower
      walking beside me.

My dear readers,

I hope
the sharing of my feelings
has helped you
to live with both
the joys and the sorrows
of your journey.

Peace & Joy,
Bob Mullin

I would be happy to hear
from you.
bob@rjmwritings.com

The willow

does not weep;

it rejoices!

Made in the USA
Middletown, DE
17 July 2016